Are you Ford or Ferrari?

Positioning Basics for Busy CEOs

Sebastian D. P. Hidalgo

Are you Ford or Ferrari?
Positioning Basics for Busy CEOs

Copyright © Sebastian D. P. Hidalgo 2024

Sebastian D. P. Hidalgo asserts the moral right to be identified as the owner of this work.

All rights reserved. No part of this publication may be reproduced, stored in a retrieval system, or transmitted, in any form or by any means without the prior written permission of the publisher, nor be otherwise circulated in any form of binding or cover other than that in which it is published and without a similar condition being imposed on the subsequent purchaser.

ISBN: 9798340426819

This book goes to God, for always giving me more than I ask and never leaving my side

Table of Contents

Don't skip this intro	1
1st Rule of Positioning	3
2nd Rule of Positioning	5
Business, not Kamasutra	8
The Sniper Mindset	14
The Positioning Triangle	29
What do you do?	34
Who do you do it for?	41
Getting Practical	51
The Positioning Task Force	54
The Role of Innovation	64
The 7 Rules of Positioning	67
Acknowledgements	68

Don't skip this intro

This book's subtitle is a promise – CEOs have no time to waste, so I won't waste yours with a long book.

But I do guarantee that you'll get the maximum value out of it.

And by the way, if you like taking notes on your books, you can find the space for it in the last pages of this volume that I set up precisely with you in mind.

But back to our topic:

Positioning should be one of the key concepts we learn in Business School, when you get a Marketing Degree, or when you complete a Sales Training.

After all, wouldn't you want to know more about the one thing that can 3x your business without any extra effort or expense?

But reality is different. Positioning is barely covered. At best, some people (even consultants who claim to help with positioning) make it an afterthought – a honorable mention.

The fact that most startup founders and many seasoned executives know little to nothing about it should also tell you why less than 50% of business survive past their first 5 years and why 90% of startups fail.

Positioning is what we'll be dealing with.

But before we go on, I need to start with a premise: This book is NOT for people who believe they have it all figured out, or who drank the Kool-Aid of their own company website claiming *"we're the leading provider in our industry."*

Likewise, this book is not for those who believe that a company is a spreadsheet, and people are just numbers that you can cross out to make ends meet.

"Are You Ford or Ferrari?" is for leaders, not for cubicle bosses. It is for those whose first priority is the customer and whose second priority is their people.

This is a book for those who want the marketplace to feel like working with them is meaningful decision – one that sends a message. Akin to buying a Ferrari.

So if that sounds like you…

Let's talk Positioning.

1st Rule of Positioning

"We are the #1 Digital Transformation provider in Europe," you could read of the website of a tech company I worked with for over two years. Around 250 employees, over $10M in ARR.

But was it true?

As I would later find out as I cut my teeth in the tech industry, that kind of claim is everywhere: IT service providers say it, AI companies say it, software development companies say it, and so on... but it's never true.

Truth be told, investors love that language and it makes for a great story to tell employees when you don't have much to say – but that little, seemingly innocent sentence on a website is actually one of the main predictors of future problems I've ever found in the industry.

It's like when a doctor watches a patient's X-Ray and there's a dark spot in a place it doesn't belong: It needs immediate attention and further analysis.

The reason?
A Positioning problem.

Much like when you hear unverified claims from a politician and realize they're desperate, fantasy claims from companies highlight two problems:

• They don't know how to communicate something that prospects can truly value

• They are lying to the prospect

You see, the company I mentioned before wasn't Accenture – it was a few hundred billions and a few thousand employees short of being Accenture.

Customers are not dumb. On the contrary: *They are sophisticated.* They read online and shop around, so when comes to your website or meets with your sales people and read false claims… there's a part of them that already doesn't trust you or any company that runs on fantasy.

And if you break the customer's trust before the interaction even starts, you can be damn sure you'll have a hard time closing them even if you're the best fit to help them.

"So how can my marketing team bridge the trust gap without lying?"

The answer to is easy: <u>You don't bridge it</u>. But why?

The answer to this second question lies in the answer to the first one: Because of Positioning.

You see, the market is like your partner when they're angry: You can't change their mind, if you ignore them they'll stay angry and if you pressure them the situation will get worse.

What we do is find an angle, establish a connection, and never break the **1st Rule of Positioning:** *Respect the customer*.

2nd Rule of Positioning

"To work on the human mind is to do good," said D.B., my Hostage Negotiation trainer, to me and twelve other students inside a cold classroom outside of Rome. The last time I saw him before that gray day in January 2024 was November 2014.

In those 10 years he'd grown gray and his health had declined, but that career he sacrificed everything for?

That had advanced so much he was getting us ready to face a delicate set of topics: Propaganda, neuropsychology and intelligence.

You're reading his words in this book because of what Positioning is. Let's establish a **definition**:

Positioning is what you do to the mind of your customers to make sure they perceive your solution as the one they need.

It is a concerted effort of Leadership, Marketing, Sales, and even Recruiting to outmaneuver your competitors.

In a nutshell, Positioning is a Business Strategy tool for market influence that the best companies in the world deploy to build trust, loyalty, and create great customer experiences.

With this definition in mind, it goes without saying that the **2nd Rule of Positioning** is to be found in D.B's words: *To work on the human mind is to do good.* Since we respect our customers, we won't craft a Positioning that's deceitful or even harmful to them.

This might seem obvious, but it's becoming less and less so as the years go by and bad actors enter every market – hence the first Rules of Positioning being about respect.

Now, Positioning might bear great financial and cultural, but...

II

It's not all sunshine and rainbows.

Positioning is hard to achieve on your own, and if you hire consultants, it requires them to do real work that doesn't end with producing a PDF report – this is why it wasn't explained to you, and the reason why the Big 4 consultant you pay $6000 per day isn't bringing it up.

In an series of interviews I conducted in 2023 with 33 tech leaders, I found that 29 of them had no idea of what Positioning was. Coincidentally, the same amount couldn't find an immediate answer to my question:

"If I was your client and I had to pick between you and a cheaper competitor that offers the same results, why would I pick your company? What makes you different?"

I added this hard data to my experience working with clients and conversations with industry peers to state the following: Finding your Positioning puts you immediately in the top 5% of businesses.

However, the fact that it is such a rarely discussed topic leads to these questions I get all the time and that I often answer in my social media content:

• Why do I even need Positioning?

• Isn't having a great sales team enough?

• What if I just invest more budget into Marketing to get more leads?

Let's answer them one by one before we sit down together for the beating heart of this book.

Business, not Kamasutra

Positioning can be perceived as an abstract concept – so much that some people, the ones with a very specific sense of humor, often go "Positioning, huh? Which *positions*?"

Funny, but as I always tell my clients and circles: **Positioning is business, not Kamasutra.**

However, the fact that something comes off as obscure enough for it to be misinterpreted is a sign, too. A sign of the fact that we need to bring it to ground level and explain it simply.

That's how we come to the questions I outlined in the previous chapter: Why do you need Positioning, and why can't you just throw more budget or better recruiting at a business problem like everyone else does?

Well, first of all, when I was a kid I remember wanting to go to a party and telling my mother "but mom, all the other kids are going!" she would always reply: *"So if all the other kids jump off a bridge, are you jumping with them?"*

Wisdom so simple it applies to business. In our case, what all the other 'kids' are doing is blindly coming at the market, attacking it either with budget, volume or talent to achieve one of the three things that Positioning affects:

- Your ability to attract the right clients
- Your ability to turn leads into deals
- Your ability to recruit top talent

All these things usually turn into more revenue and higher market share. More importantly, it translates into less stress for the leadership team, who can start focusing not just on the frustration of not meeting revenue goals or hitting a revenue ceiling, and can start working towards the company's vision.

Now, I will admit it: You *can* throw more budget, more volume or better talent at a revenue problem or at the growth ceiling you need to break through. Just like you can kick open a door, but why start kicking and risk having the neighbors call the cops on you when you could just pull down the handle and open it?

Let me explain Positioning in an even simpler metaphor – one that has found plenty of good reception among my social media following.

II

Imagine you're going on a road trip to a city you've never visited before: Positioning is to your business what Google Maps is to your trip.

Are you Ford or Ferrari?
Positioning Basics for Busy CEOs

Could you reach that same destination by guessing your way around the highway and following the road signs? *Probably yes.*

Is that the best use of your time, your fuel and your money? *Probably not.*

Now, let's say you have passengers: Would they be happier if you just got them to their destination using Google Maps, or would they prefer you drove around the highway for 3 or 4 extra hours just because you can?

You see, Positioning is exactly the same:

• As the CEO, you're the one picking the destination: This is your Vision and the strategic direction of the company.

• You have passengers who rely on you to reach that destination: These are your employees and any other stakeholders (e.g. investors).

• Just like you don't have the whole day to drive around, so you to pick the quickest, best way to get there by using Google Maps, your time and budget resources are limited, so you need Positioning to get the most results out of them with the least possible effort.

From this perspective Positioning is not just about outperforming competitors: We're actually discussing not wasting resources and maximizing the results of the ones we have. We're talking about employee satisfaction. And we're talking about a leadership team that's aligned behind one direction, with all the decrease in long meetings and difficult conversations implied in getting there.

III

Another question I often get when discussing exactly this idea is: "How is this possible? Why does Positioning matter so much, and if it matters so much, why doesn't everyone invest in it?"

The second question has an easy answer: For the same reason everyone doesn't go to the gym or eat a healthy diet. It requires commitment.

The answer to the first question is more complex, and the best source I've foud for it is the book *'Positioning - The Battle for Your Mind'* by Al Ries and Jack Trout.

The book is a visionary and foundational piece published in 1980 where the authors identify a problem: We live in an overcommunicated society where consumers are bombarded with thousands of messages every single day. The result? A defensive reaction by our brains, whereby we subconsciously filter all the information that is either irrelevant to us or doesn't stand out.

If that was reality back then, let's see together where we stand now:

- In the 1970s, people were exposed to approximately 500-1,600 advertisements per day.

• In 2007, a survey conducted on 4,000 people by the firm Yankelovich showed that number had increased to about 5,000 pieces of advertising per day.

• Finally, according to Siteefy the average person estimates to see about 10,000 ads per day.

This data is so overwhelming it becomes undeniable, so hiding behind the good old "B2B is different" excuse doesn't cut it – our potential clients are relentlessly chased around by companies of all kinds. And in this world, we're all competing for their most limited resourced: Their attention. Their *time*.

One solution to this problem is <u>Differentiation</u>. There are plenty of great examples of Differentiation in all industries, one of the most remarkable of them being the water company Liquid Death: In a market full of friendly or neutral communication, where everyone sold water in plastic bottles, they came in with an environmentalist cause and an idea to put water in metal-themed aluminum cans. They march to the sound of metal music and talk about death and murder.

Original and amazing. And yet, not everyone can do that: You don't want to be a dentist or a InsurTech company advertising using death as your theme – it would look different and it would stand out, but it would probably alienate your prospects.

The most simple example of this I can imagine is showing up at an executive networking event in a bathing suit. You would stand out and everyone would remember you, but for all the wrong reasons.

The conclusion is that Differentiation is necessary, but it's not sufficient... or at least it needs to be redefined. But I'll dedicate an entire book to this topic, so let's jump back to Positioning:

The best way to overcome the problem of an overcommunicated society is not just being different, but being relevant.

And to be relevant you have to be precise, focused and relentless.

Let's dive deeper into what that means by talking about combat sports and cars for a moment.

Are you Ford or Ferrari?
Positioning Basics for Busy CEOs

The Sniper Mindset

The year is 2015.
My 20yo self is already a combat sports fan.

It's 6am and I'm sitting in front of an old Windows laptop, eyes glued to the screen as 'the Notorious' Conor McGregor captures the UFC Championship by knocking out a legend of the sport in just 13 seconds. Joe Rogan puts a microphone in front of his face and McGregor says a quote that will forever stick with me:

"Precision beats power and timing beats speed."

Fast forward to 2024, as I re-write this book and think of the least years spent serving clients and of the last three months spent refining my own Positioning, that quote keeps coming back to me. Haunting me. Trying to tell me something.

What that quote tells me has much to do with business and Positioning, because in business the main source of power is *budget* – we use budget to hire, advertise, host events, speak at events, etc. As for speed, in business that's what everyone envies *startups* for, and what we all want and need whenever we expect results to come fast.

And precision beats power, timing beats speed, right?

The real meaning of that quote is that we can outperform our competitors, even somewhat bigger ones, regardless of how much cheaper or how established they are. All we need is to have precision and timing.

To illustrate that, I'm going to summon an example I've used in about 12 workshops – and that has solved more questions than even my best performing posts or videos.

This same example is my main answer to the false and idiotic claim every inept consultant will tell you: "We should position ourselves as…"

We don't position ourselves as anything. Remember, this is business, not the Kamasutra.

If we agree that Positioning is what you do to the mind of your customers to make sure they perceive your solution as the one they need, we can't also claim we *decide* our position in the market. Ultimately, it is our audience that holds that position, and all our work is aimed at *influencing* it.

Even when we do it perfectly, we will never own our Positioning to the point of claiming that we positioned ourselves as a leader, as luxury, or as the best.

Let's see why.

II

If I ask you to list three brands of luxury cars, there's a huge chance that your brain comes up with:

Are you Ford or Ferrari?
Positioning Basics for Busy CEOs

- Mercedes

- Porsche

- Ferrari

This is pretty straightforward. So much that you could actually tell me: "*You just proved the opposite. I see these companies as luxurious because they positioned themselves as either expensive or affordable.*"

That's because we're not done with the explanations yet: Positioning has to be relevant to a specific audience. You shouldn't give a flying *duck* about what people outside of your audience think about you.

A great example is Ford. Between late 2024 and early 2025, they're launching the *Mustang GTD*, the quickest road-going Mustang ever.

The price?
$300,000.

Even in the eyes of people who buy Ford that price point doesn't make Ford a luxury brand, let alone what it does for people who actually seek luxury. But Ford doesn't care, because they're not appealing to Porsche buyers. And have you ever seen Porsche trying to appeal to Renault drivers? Exactly.

Remember: *Precision beats power.*

Let's see how exactly that happens by going through three different scenarios together.

Scenario 1 | *Imagine your income is $45.000 USD per year.*

You're 26 years old, you like your new entry-level job and you're shopping for cars because the office is further away from your home than the previous working place, and the little 1998 compact car you bought at 19 is about to kick the bucket.

You enter the market, and these are your options:

• **Ford Fiesta** ($18.000): This car is in your range. You've been wise with your money, so you can pay it cash if you want to.

• **Toyota Rav 4** ($40.000): At more than double the price and basically costing as much as a year's worth of work, you could get a loan to buy this car... but that wouldn't be the wisest financial decision. You really want it, but you decide not to go for it.

• **Mercedes GLS** ($87.000): This is luxury for you. There's no chance you buy this, yet you promise yourself you'll get there some day.

Scenario 2 | *Your income is $200.000 USD per year.*

You climb up the corporate ladder for 10 years, and you finally get there: A corporate executive working in an office with a view. You got family now, but your income covers most expenses and you want to treat yourself.

Are you Ford or Ferrari?
Positioning Basics for Busy CEOs

You enter the market, and these are your options:

• **Ford Fiesta** ($18.000): As your income changes, so do you. Your *mindset* changes. The Fiesta is not a car you'd consider anymore – if not to give it to your daughter when she turns 18. You remember you used to have a one, but that feels like another life and another person.

• **Toyota Rav 4** ($40.000): You used to want this car, but things have changed. You gifted one to your partner when you hit that 120K/year promotion… and now you want more.

• **Mercedes GLS** ($87.000): This used to be luxury for you. Now it's as affordable as the Ford Fiesta used to be when you were 26.

However, all your colleagues love Mercedes and you see those cars every day, so they're not even special to you anymore.

And here's when something shifts:

As you can see, the Positioning of Mercedes changed… *in your mind*. Ford isn't producing worse cars than it did when you were 26, you perceive them as below your requirements and you feel like having a Ford Fiesta doesn't *say* the right thing about you. Keep this in mind.

As for the Mercedes, it's not unattainable luxury anymore. It's an everyday car. So, as humans always do, you want more.

You look further into the market:

- **Mercedes G-Wagon** ($137.000): Now this is a car you want. It's reasonable, it says about you that you're making it, you're established… yet it now feels like that Toyota Rav 4 when you were 26. Something you'll get some day, even though you could afford it now.

- **Ferrari Roma** ($280.000): This is your new version of luxury. As Mercedes becomes an everyday car, you also see people ahead of you driving supercars.

That's how you promise yourself once again that you'll make it happen and will get that Ferrari.

It's that promise that leads us to the final example:

<u>Scenario 3</u> | *Your income is $3.000.000 USD per year.*

You exit your corporate job and open a software company.

Since you read this book about Positioning in the 2020s, you're smarter than most business owners and founders and your company kills it: You're making millions and it looks like you're headed towards an exit that will retire you for good.

Once again, you want an upgrade so you enter the car market:

- **Ford Fiesta** ($18.000): You barely remember ever having one. This and a Hot Wheels car feel like the same thing to you.

- **Mercedes GLS** ($87.000): When you were 26, this was extreme luxury. At 36, it had become normality. Now that you're a millionaire and 45yo, this is the car you ended up giving your daughter when she turned 18.

- **Mercedes G-Wagon** ($137.000): This is your new normal. Your co-founders gave their partners one, so you did the same. Effortless, affordable good quality and high class.

- **Ferrari Roma** ($300.000): This is *quality*. You can afford it, and this is what you go for. But human nature hits again:

- **Koenisegg Gemera** ($2.600.000): This is now what you consider extreme quality and luxury. Even better, this is craftsmanship. Most people in the market for a Fiesta or a Toyota don't even know this exists or what is the point of paying that much for a car.

Once again, this takes the place the Mercedes GLS and the Ferrari Roma used to have in your mind. And once again, you set a new goal.

Positioning comes down to that – being in the market for long enough and with absolute consistency so your customers find you when they are ready to buy. It is about building up mental real estate in the minds of a specific target.

That mental real estate takes the form of associations: It can range from affordability to luxury, from inspiration to passion, but ultimately it comes down to one simple thing: **Trust**.

III

The first thought that will come to mind to many of the leaders reading this will be: *"But Seb, this car thing is a B2C example. In B2B things are way different."*

Yes.
But also no.
Let me explain:

First of all, all business in **H2H** (Human-to-Human) – in B2B we have this misconception that we sell to companies, when we actually sell to *people* working *in* companies. This is so true that, in a market research paper from 2021 called *'Close the expectation gap with your B2B customers'*, Deloitte claims: "B2B has always been, at its core, about people. That's why a successful petrochemicals rep knows the tensile strength specs for a particular buyer—but also knows that the buyer's baby was named after a grandmother So it's not as if relationships are new to B2B"

Second, here's how this same principle applies to B2B, and to illustrate that I'll take a real-life example:

In September 2024, I was talking to the founder of an IT consulting startup that was also getting ready to concretize their real goal: Building an AI product. The budget for development came from the IT consulting, but they wanted to scale faster so they could get ball rolling with product sooner. This founder ended up asking me: *"How do we compete against giants like Accenture and PwC?*

They are more established than us, they have bigger budgets, a better reputation."

That's how the conversation converged rapidly into B2B Positioning: "You don't," I replied with a smile.

For a moment, he was puzzled and asked me to repeat the answer. So I stared explaining.

You don't enter any market and start competing with the top dogs – that's the same mistake the company I mentioned at the beginning of the book made. I know you *want* to, because we all do and we all believe, we **know** we have a shot… but even if we did, the people that would hire Accenture and PwC would never hire a small, Germany-based team of international IT consultants, because that small team of consultants lacks the proper Positioning.

The needs of an executive that hires PwC are entirely different from the needs of a SME that hires a team like the one this founder was leading. You have to take into account that for a top executive hiring a massive consulting firm means often that the person who you think is your dream client is:

• Hiring them for a risky project and using them as collateral and scapegoat in case something goes wrong, shifting responsibility away from themselves in the eyes of the Board

• Hiring them to produce documentation that supports and helps push over the line a decision that they need someone to approve.

- Hiring a safe bet who will never be perceived as risky: If the project fails, they can say "hey, not my fault, we hired the best."

On top of that, you have to keep in mind that behind every professional decision there is a p*ersonal motive* – which is why all business is H2H and we sell to people in companies.

For instance, when that small team of IT consultants walks in trying to steal a gig from PwC or Accenture, they could lack both the full picture and the experience to imagine it: Perhaps the CEO of the company is about to step down, so the CTO or CIO who hired the IT consultants needs to invest in a project that drives a significant ROI to the company… so that they can get the Board's favor and maybe get a shot at becoming the new CEO.

And that's just the politics side of things. On the other end of the spectrum there is the project management aspect: Is a small team of IT consultants ready for a $2M scope? Can they handle a chain of command made of 20 people who all want to have a say in the project? Can they deliver under pressure, or under the expectations of stakeholders who barely have the time to meet them often?

You see, in B2B this Positioning thing, when you get it wrong, is the equivalent of going to 26yo you from the cars example and trying to sell them a Ferrari Roma. Or going to your 45yo executive self and trying to get them to trade in their Ferrari Roma for that same Ford Fiesta: You'll end up looking out of place, sounding out of place, and inevitably you'll get so used to targeting the wrong audience that at some point you'll go: "I need a sale, here's the Ferrari for the price of a Ford."

What happens then is that, even if you do have a Ferrari and make it cheap for the 26yo, nobody will trust you because you're selling it at a price point that signals there's something wrong with it. So you get desperate and decide to stop selling just Ferraris, and start selling Fords because you need money – and you do close enough sales to get by, but that came with a price because you lose the trust of your customers.

You lost it in two stages: The moment you tried to sell to the wrong audience, because they were never supposed to be your customers to begin with, and the moment your real audience finally noticed you but saw you running round as lost as Tarzan if you put him in New York City.

The final result is that your real ideal customer, the one who could've afforded a Ferrari, the one you could've targeted from the very beginning, now saw you selling Fords and thinks you're phony.

That's the outcome of trying to sell at a premium to an audience hunting for discounts. And it's no different if you try to sell cheap to an audience that values premium, because t*he point is never what you sell but what the people you sell to value.*

So, how do you avoid making this mistake? And even if you do avoid it, how do you build trust with the right audience?

That's our next point. Because remember: It's not just how precision beats power... it's about how *timing beats speed*.

IV

An overcommunicated society and wrong or generic targeting aren't the only problems SMEs are facing right now – there are two that make everything way worse:

• According to the Ehrenberg-Bass Institute's research for the LinkedIn B2B Institute, **only 5% of businesses** are in the market for most goods and services at any one time

• Per Dr. Jeremy Lent, you need to connect with a prospect **a minimum of seven times within an 18-month period** to penetrate their consciousness enough to become a viable alternative they will consider.

Now, solutions will change according to who you ask: These very trendy "lead generation" agencies will tell you that you address these problems by blasting thousands of emails per week until you hit the 5%. A CMO will tell you that you need more awareness campaigns. A Sales specialist or a closer will insist you just need to invest in more sales training so you can just brute force your way into deals.

There's truth to each of these options – but there's also a way you can take to make the process smoother and easier: Positioning.

You see, in an overcommunicated society where everyone is fighting for our customers' limited attention, if we truly are to win their trust and get them on a sales interaction, we need to achieve three things:

- **Create a concise messaging:** This is not Marketing or PR advice. Your messaging is a factor that should start at the Leadership level and then trickle downstream into the organization. Creating concise messaging means having a deep knowledge of your customers (and your traditional "client avatar" little diagrams won't help here), your competitors, the market, and your competitive advantages.

- **Broadcast it consistently:** Everything you do is broadcasting. Every meeting you attend, every event you go to, every case study you publish and every sales interaction. The message has to be consistent to avoid confusion: If you take into account that 97% of the addressable market isn't ready to buy at any point, becoming extremely consistent is a must because, by the time they're ready, you can't afford to confused prospects. If they don't understand what you do, who you do it for and why it matters? They will buy from competitors because they won't see themselves in your solution.

- **Connect with our ideal customers:** This

involves talking to current customers and potential ones. Having someone in your team that understands the trends prospects pay attention to, the sources they trust and what they are trying to achieve in business. Positioning is about connection – at the cost of sounding Pavlovian, I'll say that Positioning is about creating and reinforcing neural pathways that link your business to their needs.

Precision happens through your messaging. The timing takes place between broadcasting and connection – andIf you achieve these three things, and I do understand that doing it on your own is easier said than done, by the time someone jumps on a call with you, *you will already have their trust*.

And at that point, closing the deal and starting a relationship as their provider of choice will be a matter of agreeing on a price and timeline.

A well-positioned company is like a sniper: They sit at the right place, at the right angle, and pull the trigger at the right moment.

Which leads me to close this chapter with the **4th Rule of Positioning:** *Think like a sniper*.

Now, you're all caught up with the theory.

Let's move things into a more practical side: What are the in & outs of finding your Positioning? And how can you do it without investing too much of your time?

Are you Ford or Ferrari?
Positioning Basics for Busy CEOs

It all starts with finding an answer to the three most important questions in business.

The Positioning Triangle

Most companies exist in the market following a trifecta: Product, Service and Price.

Nothing wrong with it at first sight, right? *Right*.

Or at least, nothing until you realize that this might've worked up until 1982 or, at best, 1992 – when you could run a company in a vacuum. Find a market, create a product for them, serve them at the best of your ability, then keep selling to others in that same market. Easy peasy lemon squeezy.

In 2024, things are different. Your customers have infinite choices: They can pick service providers or products from any location around the planet, delivered by teams that can be 100x cheaper than you, or 100x more expensive. Every year new competitors pour in, and in the last three years those competitors have become more nimble and agile, powered by AI's ability to augment human effort.

The most common result of this situation is a world where thousands of companies across all industries end up competing for price, hitting a descending spiral that always ends at the same miserable destination.

In a market like this, we don't compete by trying the same business model over and over again:

We need to change the trifecta. We need to go from Product, Service and Price – *a model of assumptions* and educated guesses that takes out of the equation competitive advantages, value propositions, and even the customer – to *a **model of insight*** built on the answers to three questions that make up the Positioning Triangle:

- What do you do?

- Who do you do it for?

- Why does it matter?

This is extremely simple, I know, but simplicity is one of the hardest things to achieve. Simplicity requires mastery and it is the result of sophistication.

To prove this point, I'm about to invite you to a challenge. Based on the results of said challenge, I will make a few educated guesses and safe predictions about your business.

II

The first half of the challenge is for you directly. I need you to grab a pen or, if you don't have one, your cell phone. Then write down either on a piece of paper, on this book or on your notes app the answer to the following question:

Why should your clients pick you over a competitor that's cheaper, or one that has better proof and more time on the market? What makes your business different?

If you don't have a clear answer to this question, or if it takes you more than 3 minutes to come up with one, you belong to the >90% of business owners and leaders who have a Positioning problem.

Now, onto the next challenge – the one you will need other people for. More specifically, you need to summon, call or message:

- Two people out of your Leadership team
- Three people out of Marketing
- Three people from Sales

To each of them, ask this simple question:

"What does our company do, and why is it better than what our competitors do?"

There are two requirements to make this experiment: The first one is that you answer that question first, in no more than two or three short sentences; the second is that you ask this question to each of them separately. Remember to record the answers.

Now, onto the results and what they mean.

In total, you will have nine answers: The experiment is a success if *at least 6 of them give you the same exact answer*.

On the contrary, the experiment is a failure if they give answers that are vague, unspecific, or generic – e.g. saying that your biggest advantage is your people, or the fact that you're #1 in the market.

Here's how the results will look for readers of this

book:

• About 95 leaders out of 100 who read this work on Positioning won't have an immediate answer to the first question.

• In 99% of cases, their teams will fail the second experiment.

If this sounds like you, you have a Positioning issue that's either keeping your growth stagnant, or actively hurting you (you've missed revenue for more than one quarter, or your cashflow is irregular).

Here are other common symptoms:

- Your Leadership team sometimes takes longer than you like in making decisions.
- Your Marketing and Sales teams don't communicate much between each other – if they even communicate at all.
- Your employees aren't very invested in what the company does, and since they can't explain it properly, they rarely generate interest in it.
- When hiring, you often lose great talent to bigger competitors even if your compensation package is good.
- You don't generate enough new clients
- You struggle closing existing clients

Overall, if you're having some or all of these symptoms, a safe prediction to make is that in the near future you will worry about where the cashflow is going to come from – and that you're either already starting to or will soon consider expanding your product/service portfolio in a bid to cast a wider net and generate more cashflow.

That's all preventable through Positioning.

But now that we diagnosed the disease, it's time to find a cure.

What do you do?

Finding an answer to this question is probably the easiest part of the equation, even though it can get tricky.

If your communication has been chronically inconsistent, understanding what exactly you do is the first obstacle to overcome – the second being how you communicate that to your ideal customer.

When you ask most people "what do you do?" they will respond with a statement that goes:

I'm a [ROLE] at a company in the [INDUSTRY] that sells [PRODUCT/SERVICE].

If you ask people what their company does, they will say another templatized statement like:

We provide [PRODUCT/SERVICE] to companies in [INDUSTRY].

If you were to get more inquisitive, in both cases you would start getting long-winded, complex description of what these people and their companies do. And the more you let them talk, the more confusing things will get because they'll start introducing jargon and technical words until you're left with: *"Ah, so you're a [INDUSTRY] company!"*

They will happily nod, confirm and you'll walk away with negative interest in whatever it is that they do… because they didn't actually tell you.

The sin here is not lack of expertise, but *too much* of it and an extreme eagerness to share it. To show everyone how innovative, how technically sound and how professional their business is.

The sad reality is that your prospects don't care about your processes until they're on a sales call with you – if ever. What they care about is the result, and that's where we have to have a mindset shift:

The first step of presenting what we do to others in a way that gets them interested is to start talking about the outcomes we provide, not the inputs we use to provide it.

Here we come to **Rule #5 of Positioning:** *Start from within.*

This rule matters because the first thing you need to get clarity on is what is it that you do, meaning:

- What is our type of service called?

- What is the results we give to customers?

- What difference do those results make in their life?

- What's the best transformation we can provide to a customer, if everything works perfectly?

- What is the process we use to get them to that result?

Ideally, what you want here is to shift how you speak both internally and externally. When thinking about what you do, shift the focus from the job position or the category you're in to the results you provide:

For example, you're not an end-to-end provider of Digital Transformation – that's so broad it means very little even to people who know the industry. What you *can* be, however, is a tech company who decreases operational costs for clients by over 40% per year by automating their analog processes.

Now, *that* sounds sexy, We have a quantifiable number. Doesn't that sound like something someone you know would be interested in?

It does, but it's not enough, because there are other companies who do the same. So even though we are promising a result and getting people interested, we still need to find a position in their minds that's strong enough for them to pick us.

That's why part of getting clear about what you do is explaining how you do it and how you do it different than anybody else.

And for that we need to look at our competitors.

II

One of the main reasons why companies can't seem to find proper Positioning is a phenomenon, or perhaps an *disease*, that I've decided to call **Benchmark Slavery**.

You've encountered it before, but haven't seen it. To be honest, I hinted at it at the start of the book, and again when talking about the team of IT consultants trying to compete against Accenture for clients:

The reason most companies write claims like *"the leading company in..."* or *"the #1 provider of..."* is the same reason why they think they can compete with market leaders that don't even know they exist: **They copy them**.

Benchmark Slavery is common aberration of benchmark analysis. It happens when instead of taking your competitors and using them as an example of what not to do or what to do differently, you end up looking at the companies they work with and the revenue they bring in and think:

"They must be doing something right. I better copy them, so I can get the same clients they do."

But here's the thing: The #1 companies in your market? They know their Positioning. That's why they got where they are. So thinking you can copy them and achieve similar results is an understandable logical fallacy you will often find your Marketing and Sales teams pushing for under the guise of sentences like "we need to position ourselves as trusted partners."

However, the issue is the fact that it's your market-dominant competitors mastered their own Positioning.

More often than not, you can't theirs without taking a look under the hood, and you haven't even developed your own – so trying to copy them is like watching Mike Tyson videos and thinking you can beat professional heavyweights just by copying Mike's moves.

Unadvisable to say the least, and if you tried you'd soon find yourself lying flat on a canvas under bright lights, knocked out cold. The business version of that is finding yourself struggling to meet revenue goals, or hitting a ceiling you don't know how to break past.

The nightmare version of it is you having to terminate people and, eventually, the company you've devoted so much to.

So this begs the question, how do you do competitor analysis correctly?

Or, let's be realistic, how do you teach people in your teams to do it properly?

III

Doing competitor analysis will have your people turning into investigative journalists – you find a red thread to pull from, and you patiently pull it until you reach deeper and deeper layers into your competitor's business.

It starts with the targeting: Pick companies who are actual competitors. If you have an AI consulting firm for the public sector, search for others that have:

- Similar employee count

- Same target customer
- Similar turnover

Then you want to pick at least two smaller competitors, and at least two that sit at around double your size: This should give you a comprehensive overview of the market.

From there, start with a top-down approach and analyze their:

- **Social media:** What type of content do they post, and who engages with it? Do their customers participate in conversations?

- **Corporate influencers:** Do they have an active CEO on socials? Who engages with them, and what are the conversations about? How often do they post, and what do they talk about?

- **Website:** How is it structured? Does it serve a purpose, and is it likely to be generating results for them? What's their main focus on the homepage?

- **Testimonials:** What do the testimonials say, what's said between the lines, and what's not said? Testimonials can be an opportunity to find out not just what your ideal customers consider to be good service, but also what areas your competitor is not covering that you could cover.

- **Products & Services:** Do they promise any results, and if so which ones? Are they better or worse than yours? Are they slow, fast, or boutique? What *don't* they cover in their offering?

- **Case studies:** What do they highlight about their products and services? How do they present them? Is this a strong area for them or a weakness?

- **Publications:** All companies put out there free value for people to dowload. What are they publishing? What topics does it cover?

- **PR:** Are their employees or the company as a whole featured in industry papers? If so, which ones?

Use industry leaders as a real benchmark, because they will often be very good at discussing topics their audience (your audience) cares about.

However, keep your focus on your real competitors – once you'll be done uncovering what they do and how they do it, you'll be surprised to find out that there are gaps and cracks.

This all leads me to the **6th Rule of Positioning:** *Play to your strengths & frame their weaknesses.*

Remember, this is not something you do – as a CEO, you have enough on your plate. I often go through this process *for* clients if their team is small, but in most cases I help them build a team that works with me during the entire re-positioning process.

I call that type of team a Task Force, and I will explain later how can you build one.

Who do you do it for?

B2B is behind.
Behind in Marketing, behind in Sales.

It's nobody's fault except for the usual "B2B is different" excuse, and for the fact that plenty of people working in B2B stop progressing in their chosen field the moment they stop studying and walk through your company's door.

This is not a rant, by the way – it's an assessment of one simple reality: All it takes is listening to a B2B workshop, sitting down in a B2B sales call or looking at a B2B website to realize that the only thing we seem to be able to talk about is ourselves.

In the past three or four years, I've seen companies use their one-pagers and sales assets to brag about everything from how many awards they've received and how great of a working place they are, to how many locations they've opened and how many employees they've hired. And don't get me wrong, all those things are *great*... if you are looking for investors or for an exit. They're pretty much useless if your goal is to get clients, and they're a major symptom of a Positioning problem:

In B2B, most companies lost or never acquired the ability to speak to the expectations and needs of their clients.

And that's exactly what you're seeing whenever you open a competitor website and all they can talk about is themselves and their company, instead of addressing how they could transform their customer's.

The answer to the question *"Who do you do it for?"* is perhaps one of the most important things you will compile in business, because it's not just about creating a fancy customer avatar using templates from HubSpot or any other sales platform. Listing out a couple of pain and gains onto a document that will get forgotten by everyone is not the solution – just like the solution isn't to go full 1995 and start building out demographic profiles:

- Education level
- Job position
- Age group
- Location
- Income
- Gender

There is some value to this, but it's barely the foundation. What we need to tackle when talking about who we serve is psychographics: Or, in layman's terms, all the things that will allow us to overcome skepticism and establish trust with these people.

From this perspective, the Positioning way of going about business prioritizes relationship and trust over transaction – something that shouldn't anyway be a problem if we consider that a B2B sales cycle can last up to 6 months. Our goal with

Positioning is being less Ford and more Ferrari – being more desirable, more noticeable, less taken for granted. It is about putting yourself in the right position to establish trust beforehand, and t reduce the timeframes while increasing the perceived value.

With this goal in mind, let's talk *psychographics*. A select group of people from your Marketing and Sales teams should work *together* in order to uncover the nitty-gritty of your ideal customer.

II

I want to paint a very clear picture of this, so let's start with an **example**:

Imagine you are running proprietary algorithms for data produced by sensors on vehicles, and your ideal customer is the Fleet Manager of an ambulance fleet at a hospital. Their direct boss is the hospital's Director of Operations, they themselves manage a small team, and they have tried, unsuccessfully, a couple of digitalization initiatives,

Here's how create a basic Ideal Customer Profile, or ICP:

Goals

Just like you, your ideal customers have goals – and behind every professional goal there's a personal one.

According to who you are targeting, current goal could be to grow the company, to stop feeling pressure from the Board, or to get a promotion.

Behind those goals there could be anything from having bragging rights during Golf on Sundays, feeling accepted by the rest of their Management team, to having the luxury of being able to take time off and focus completely on being with their family.

In the specific case of your Fleet Manager, his professional goal aligns with that of their boss: Having an easy way to manage their fleet, with less stress and more precision, so that reporting to Management becomes seamless.

Their personal goals might be quite different – they're probably seeking a pay upgrade, or perhaps thet're aiming at becoming Director of Operations when their current boss changes roles.

To achieve that, they start looking at companies like yours – the AI-based data-processing company.

Desired state

Your ideal customer's desired state can be an aspiration, but it is often a need – they want to achieve a transformation or reach a goal, and it usually looks like taking their company, their team or their career from point A to point B.

For example, your Fleet Manager wants to have a clear, real-time overview of all vehicle available, their current state, their need for maintenance, and their readiness to operate.

Ideally, they want to see all of that from a dashboard that even a non-technical person can take a look at, and weekly reports have to be automated.

Current state

Your ideal customer's current state is reality – here they are having all sorts of issues, delays and unexpected events that get in the way of their goals.

They know things are not as smooth as they should be, and they're probably aware of competitors doing better than them.

For your Fleet Manager, the current state looks a lot like their day-to-day at work: Slow processes, putting out fires constantly, the occasional human error like thinking an ambulance is ready to go but finding out it isn't.

If you don't know the current state of your ideal customer, you can't show them you empathize with their problem – which also means you can't show them you understand it or know how to solve it.

Real & perceived obstacles

The obstacles are part of reality, but they are a part of reality your ideal customer doesn't really grasp.

Real obstacles are the problems *you*, the expert company, know they have but are unaware of.

Perceived obstacles are those problems they know they have and think are the reason why they're actually seeking help from a provider.

Let's go back to our Fleet Manager. They might believe that lack of digitalization is what's causing their problems, when in fact their real problem is that their team has resisted even minimal automation efforts.

Their real obstacle is *culture* – and that's an opportunity for you, the service provider, to educate your ideal customer about how every digital transformation is as much about culture and adoption as it is about technology and systems.

Making the Fleet Manager aware of that won't only position you as an authority in their mind compared to a company that only talks about processes and features, but it will also increase your value in the Fleet Manager's eyes, immediately setting you apart from competitors.

Expectations

Expectations are often to be found in industry

standards and experiences with previous providers. They are the playground in which you should set your competitive advantage:

If your ideal customer has been conditioned to expect something in a long timeframe, you can break that belief and achieve a prime position in their mind by proving you've done it faster, with equal or better results.

In our example, our Fleet Manager was expecting just technology out of working with a service provider – nobody ever told them it was about culture, so you have a chance to disrupt that expectation and gifting them an epiphany moment about why their transformation initiatives haven't been sticking.

Whatever your competition conditioned your customers to expect, in Positioning becomes our tool to turn the tables by offering something *different*.

Limitations

I have never met a company with an infinite budget, and I believe you haven't either: Limitations are the real-life constraints your ideal customer has.

For our Fleet Manager, depending on the size of the hospital, they will have budget limitations, timeframe limitations, and decision-making limitations.

If you know these in advance and talk to them in

your Sales/Marketing efforts, your ideal customer will see you as the go-to – someone that understands not just the technical side and their needs, but the realistic boundaries of the project at hand.

Influencers

No, I'm not referring to 20-something-yo girls on Instagram building a travel blog. By *"influencers"* I mean every personality, institution, publication or association that your ideal customer follows and listens to.

These can be websites, magazines, podcasts, CEOs of other companies, and so on.

You need to know who and what these are, because each one of them is your shot at being seen with those people, speaking on those platforms or writing in those publications.

You want to be visibile, but if you're selling to ambulance Fleet Managers, there's no use in you being visible to janitors or university professors – you need to be in front of the people and platforms your ideal customers pay attention to.

Circles

One of the most common mistakes I've seen is how companies will pay tens of thousands to speak at events and have booths at fairs… of their own industry.

Don't get me wrong, there is plenty of value to

that, but your chances of it impacting your revenue punchline are small.

Your ideal customer's circles are all the online and offline communities and events your ideal customer hangs out at.

Your company needs to be visible there – not just at events full of providers who do more or less the same things you do.

III

All of this brings me to the most important point in this book: *The final rule of Positioning*. And I chose to put it last because that's where Strategic Positoning ends and Tactical Positioning begins.

Much like the world didn't stop, end and implode when God finished creation on the 7th day, finding and finalizing your Positioning is the start – a *new* start, to be specific, which is why I refer to my work with clients as 'transformation.'

There's nothing simpler yet deeper than the **7th Rule of Positioning**: *Is it about the customer?*

As you can see, the rule is a question. That's by design, because "Is it about the customer?" is what you and your teams, from Management to Operations – heck, even your cleaning personnel if you ask me – should be asking whenever thinking about something new.

The 7th Rule of Positioning contains also the answer for the third question of the Positioning

Triangle, because the moment you know every detail about what you do, what your clients need and how you deliver it differently is also the moment you find out **why it matters** – to them.

New copy for the website?
Has to be about the customer.

New sales approach?
Has to be about the customer.

New features?
They have to be about the customer.

The customer is the beginning and the end of our business. The alpha and the omega – if we can't attract them, we don't get paid. If we can't retain them, we will go down (along with our reputation).

Positioning, ultimately, is a customer-centric and competitor-savvy approach to doing business.

But why do most companies fail at it?
And how can you create your own?

Let's close this book with those answers.

Getting Practical

You know your expertise is versatile.

As a matter of fact, I'm sure that your business could help most businesses on the planet with the results you provide – am I wrong?

But here's the thing: When we try to appeal to everyone, no one listens. But we sill don't want to leave money on the table, so what do we do? We start doing our best to make our Positioning as broad as we can.

We even introduce new products and services that accommodate a plethora of different needs.

If you've been there, you're not alone – most companies end up exactly in that spot. I have been in that spot – in the no man's land where the marketplace looks and sounds like a fruit market where all merchants scream so loud your brain tunes them out one by one.

But why does this happen?
Why can't companies just focus?
Why can't our messaging just be precise?

The answer is in two cognitive biases: **Solomon's Paradox** and the **Curse of Knowledge**.

Solomon's Paradox is the common thing we're all familiar with: You always have better advice and are wiser for other than you do for yourself. The Curse of Knowledge, instead, happens when we know so much about a topic that we end up assuming that everyone understands it the same way we do, and communicate accordingly.

These two cognitive biases don't affect just individuals: When people within a team spend weeks, months and years working together, they gradually start developing similar ideas, common perspectives and shared biases. In psychology this is called *groupthink* – and it can take quite extreme forms, but in a business concept the main side effect of this is the incapacity to find or see the correct decisions.

The combination of these three factors is quite common. In the coaching industry, it is not unusual for a coach to have a coach, just like every therapist is required to have a therapist. As humans, we need each other. More importantly, we need *objective* others. In business, that same combination of psychological factors makes it difficult to find your own Positioning because:

- There are too many interests at stake
- You and your team lack diverse perspectives
- You know too much
- You are too busy

Mind you – it's not *impossible* to find your Positioning on your own. It could just take more months than you have or want.

The easiest path to finding your company's Positioning and break past revenue ceilings or start meeting your revenue goals, the best solution is to bring in an external. Someone who won't be afraid to tell the truth, challenge anything in the current state of the company, and mediate between different ideas to achieve a common alignment on a new direction for your company.

Even then, a common concern executives and leaders have is time: *"Okay, we're hiring a consultant, but who has time for all these workshops, meetings, and reading documentation?"*

That's a common concern, and one of the most legitimate ones. Over the past three years, one of the best ways I've found to deal with the time issues goes beyond just doing more with less when it comes to workshops – it's about building a team you can delegate the Positioning process to.

Here's how.

Are you Ford or Ferrari?
Positioning Basics for Busy CEOs

The Positioning Task Force

Positioning is something you cannot delegate to B players. Full disclosure, even if your company is packed with A players, it might not be enough – Positioning is work you delegate to people who have decisional power and organizational influence.

But it's not just a matter of job titles, either. It has plenty to do with personality, too. People inside your Task Force eed to be:

- Committed to improving the company
- Willing to disagree when need be
- Dedicated to excellence
- Willing to communicate

The last point is paramount.

The worst mistake people make in communication is thinking that communication actually happened. To avoid it, the people you pick for the Task Force need to be willing to have conversations and to collaborate – even if they come from "rival" teams like Sales and Marketing.

Let's explore more key features of this group.

II

Hiearchy | The Task Force works best in organizations where people are already used to an accountability structure. And even if your company practices "flat hierarchies," the people inside the Task Force need to stick to one.

My framework of choice is the DACI, where you have the following roles:

- **Driver** | This is the project lead. It *can* be you as CEO if you have time to attend weekly or bi-weekly meetings, but it *must* be someone else if you don't.

In my projects, the Driver is the key point of contact between myself and the rest of the team, so they need to be available. They also are charged with leading the team.

This person's key professional requirement is that they know the in and outs of the business. Personality-wise, they must be a great communicator, have empathy and good observational skills. They are also the "accountability partners" of everyone else in the Task Force.

- **Approver** | This is often the CEO. When the CEO is too busy even for this role, they assign it to someone who is already used to making important decisions.

The Decider is empowered to approve or reject proposals and suggest changes of direction. They are also takes with getting additional approval from stakeholders external to the Task Force, such as team leads or heads of department.

In terms of personality, you'll want in this role someone decisive and determined rather than someone who needs plenty of time to ponder.

• **Contributor** | The Task Force can't be filled with Senior Execuives only, for it is supposed to be a cross-functional team of perspectives and roles.

To avoid blindspots, here's where we introduce diversity: Unlike it happens for the Driver and the Approver, you can have multiple stakeholders in the role of Contributors. They should come from Marketing, Sales, IT, Product and/or Customer Experience.

The priority here goes to customer-facing stakeholders – first and foremost.

   • **Informed** | These are people you might need input or approval from, but who did not make it into the core team.

In bigger companies this is often you – the CEO – all you have is no more than one or two hours per month to dedicate to a Positioning transformation.

III

Team Size | Despite its cool name, the Task Force looks less than a full military department, and much more like a Special Operations unit: You can't have too many people in it.

Should you let too many be part of this group, they would slow down decisions and we would risk your Positioning becoming the product of committee mindset.

For this reason, the sweet spot of a Positioning

Task Force is a team that has at least three people, but no more than five or even six, in extreme cases.

If we start looking at a Task Force of nine people or more, we're killing the project before it starts.

IV

Comms Network | Your Comms Network are all the stakeholders that need to be on top of the process, but can't and won't be in your Task Force.

These people should know who the Decider is, and the Decider should check in with them on a fixed cadence to make sure they're up to date with the process.

Usually, those who will be part of this network are people with power to make decisions. If anyone in your organization has veto power but no time to partake in any stage of the Positioning process, they should be considered as part of the Comms Network.

V

As the CEO, your Task Force will be the best way to go through the Positioning work without having to invest more than a few hours per month.

Some CEOs want to be more hands-on, others less. A few usually will have a monthly call with me, and one with their Decider – and that's it.

Even if you're not engaged with an external and

decide to go about your Positioning internally, it's important that you do build a Task Force and that the project becomes a priority for them.

And yet, here's where I get another question:

"What does the result of Positioning look like?"

The End Result

Positioning is data-driven alchemy.

You start with the raw materials: You take all the information you have about yourself, your competitive advantage, the value you provide to customers, your competitors and even what you stand for as a company.

Then, through a process of distillation and purification, you refine everything into the clearest and simplest form you can attain.

The end result of alchemy is gold.
The end result of Positioning is… gold.

Usually, more revenue, smoother decisions.
Less headaches in your free time. Better culture.

But that's still abstract.
Let's get granular.

Positioning results in something my clients in Tech love: **Dashboards**. Living, ever-evolving data pools where anyone in the relevant roles can access, with just a few clicks, all the information they need about how to talk to customers, how to respond to objections, how to improve the selling process.

It also results in something that all my clients working in more customer-facing roles and companies love equally: **Statements**.

Simple ways to communicate the complexity of your company in a way that just *clicks* with your ideal customers.

Once you get to the end result of Positioning, you will feel accomplished and satisfied... but also surprised.

Surprised that so much information had to go into putting out simple, clear datasets that help you sell more, charge more, and reduce sales cycles.

Surprised that you didn't invest in that before, and that you're walking into industry events and customer meetings with newfound confidence.

Surprised that your culture rallies around the same ideas, easily, and that your employees start turning into one of the few and actual brand awareness tools that you need.

I could give you frameworks for this: Statements, formulas, templates – but I won't, because working Positioning Statements without doing the Positioning work is like putting on a suit of fake muscles and expecting to be able to bench press 300lbs without ever having entered a gym.

However, what I *will* give you is a story.

One example of this "surprise effect" that Positioning grants you in unexpected area is a company we will call Data Ventures LLC:

They were selling data processing software to aerospace companies. They also worked for other the public sector. For Data Ventures LLC, business was going as well as it goes when you keep winning government bids, but they had a Positioning issue hidden under a recruiting pain: They struggled to attract top talent – a big issue considering that they were growing their customer base.

There were many ways to solve this issue. One of them was, of course, throwing budget at it. The other was finding the root cause of their problem, and then creating a cure.

It didn't take long for Data Ventures to realize something interesting: There were very few people excited to work on public sector projects – and I'm told that's a common recruiting pain point in their niche. But also, they soon realized that there were very few companies in that niche working with aerospace companies.

So we came up with a thesis: What if we hit recruiting events and instead of talking about how impactful our solutions are in reducing the time clerks need to work through paperwork... we talk about our latest space project?

This thesis was a zero-risk proposition because Data Ventures had already paid for at least three recruitment fairs.

The results were astounding: Not just the faces of potential candidates lit up when they heard names like the European Space Agency, but they started applying for jobs. And the icing on the cake?

A good number of those applicants were women.

Data Ventures LLC was stuck.
Their saving grace?

Are you Ford or Ferrari?
Positioning Basics for Busy CEOs

A Business Strategy concept that ended up affecting not just how potential customers saw them (after all, who wouldn't trust a company that has the trust of an industry where the highest standards are the norm?), but also how the top talent they weren't able to attract perceived them.

You see, in business sometimes all we need is an original idea – it can come from a new hire, or from a consultant. It can even come from your COO taking a month-long vacation and coming up with enough clarity to see problems for what they are.

Regardless of who brings forth that change, what remains true is that often in business we find ourselves spinning our wheels, trying to get out of situations we found ourselves in by just trying to do our best.

There's nothing wrong with being stuck, just like nothing wrong with being disconnected from our customers or copying our competitors – that's how over 90% of businesses end up.

What *is* wrong is staying there just because we think of ourselves as the kind of leaders who have to figure it out on their own.

What *is* wrong is normalizing your revenue problems, be it a dip or a plateau, to the point we let them take us away while we're having lunch with our spouses or spending time with our little ones.

In the puzzle of things that make up a successful business, Positioning is not the panacea that will cure all your ailments.

But I can guarantee you it can get rid of plenty of growing pains. All thanks to an idea – a new perspective, a novel frame.

And here's the last question I'd like to answer: *"Is Positioning about innovation?"*

The Role of Innovation

It's easy to fall into the trap of thinking Positioning is about innovating. About finding something extremely new, shocking, revolutionary.

And don't get me wrong, in some cases it is:

• When OpenAI launched ChatGPT, it immediately propelled them to industry leader status because they did what Jack Trout and Al Ries, the authors of *"Positioning - The Battle for Your Mind"* describe as the ideal condition: They were first in the market.

• When Liquid Death disrupted the water market, they were far from first but they were defiantly different: A decision that made them the favorite case studies of many marketers out there.

But building another ChatGPT is no easy feat, and we've covered most industries don't let themselves to what Liquid Death did.

Innovation matters. My entire consulting process, which I love to call the *Neural Network Approach*, is built with innovation in mind: It implements an Agile mindset and framework into traditional Management Consulting combined with Business Strategy and other disciplines, with one goal in mind: Impacting not just one area of the business but the entire system, with minimal friction and maximum results.

However, I am aware that not all innovation is necessary or even useful: We have little use for a

Boeing 747 that comes equipped with a honk, just like we could built a bottle with holes or a phone without screen. The Tesla Model 3 that could produce farting sound was hilarious, but that was pretty much all the use that feature had.

So they are all novel ideas, none of them useful.

Positioning is more about *strategy*, and strategy means taking guided action based on a decision to play games you can win.

Positioning is about *framing* – about finding the weaknesses in a system (like the market and your competitors) and inserting yourself in that gap.

Ultimately, however, Positioning is about making business what it always was: *Connection and trust*.

If there's anything you take away from this book, let that be the importance of connecting with your customers. Of putting them first, talking directly at their most relevant needs.

I'm not saying "don't think about profit." My argument is actually that there's plenty of profit to be made once we understand the correlation between the quality and impact of our service, and the amount of profit we generate. And the only way to create that impact is to build that connection with the people on the other side of those corporate logos and shiny job titles.

You will maximize your upside once you let prospects finally understand how you maximize theirs, and how you do that differently from every single alternative in the market.

The title of this book is "Are You Ford or Ferrari?" not because I don't believe in the value of a reliable, affordable car, or because I believe that luxury is the final destination.

As our markets get more and more competitive, as the entry bar lowers and everyone starts fighting for breadcrumbs, being less Ford and more Ferrari means something way more existential: It means becoming synonym with an outcome. With a certain level of quality and craftmanship.

Being less Ford and more Ferrari means understanding that excellence is a commitment, and making it the standard at which your company operates from Leadership and Culture to Sales, Marketing and Customer Success.

Being less Ford and more Ferrari is about standards, and I apply those from the words I publish to the people in my tribe.

I will never align with the bureaucrat CEO who spent 30 years at a Big 4 consulting firm, and at the first sign of a revenue dip starts firing people as if they were numbers on a spreadsheet.

My tribe are of leaders that are always looking for more, that won't settle for anything less than fulfilled clients and that care about building a culture where people feel a sense of safety, purpose and impact.

So if you're in my tribe, I want to dedicate this book to you. Thank you for reading.

The 7 Rules of Positioning

Rule #1
Respect the customer

Rule #2
To work on the human mind is to do good

Rule #3
Precision beats power, timing beats speed.

Rule #4
Think like a sniper

Rule #5
Start from within

Rule #6
Play to your strengths & frame their weaknesses

Rule #7
Is it about the customer?

Are you Ford or Ferrari?
Positioning Basics for Busy CEOs

Acknowledgements

I'll live and die by one sentence: Excellence is a commitment. The book you're reading right now is proof – I re-wrote it from scratch after doing more work with clients, and after refining my own Positioning through my mentor.

Which brings me to the next point: You never achieve excellence alone. The fact this book exists at all is something I owe to my friend Bronté Graham Sr. He's the one who pushed me to use my writing background to put my knowledge on these page.

Another special thanks will go to the people who made this second version possible by blessing me with the knowledge, like my clients, and the guidance, like my mentor Torrey Dawley. Hard to tell where I'd be if I didn't work with him.

The artist behind the book cover is none other than Chad Jordan – a design superstar that I'm honored to call a friend. Thanks for being part of this.

The main requirements to write a book are health, time and peace of mind – three things I owe to God, to whom this book is dedicated.

Finally, this acknowledgement is for you, the reader: Whether you're a friend, an employee, a podcast guest or a current or future client, the fact that you took the time to read this means the world to me.

Contact

If you want to get in touch with me, the best way to find me is probably through social media.

Scan the QR Code below to connect with me on **LinkedIn**, and shoot me a message – I'm pretty responsive and would he happy to hear from you.

www.ingramcontent.com/pod-product-compliance
Lightning Source LLC
Chambersburg PA
CBHW070355230526
45471CB00006B/2584